LIKE A SEA

Winner of the IOWA POETRY PRIZE

LIKE A SEA

SAMUEL AMADON

UNIVERSITY OF IOWA PRESS, IOWA CITY

University of Iowa Press, Iowa City 52242
Copyright © 2010 by Samuel Amadon
www.uiowapress.org
Printed in the United States of America

Design by Richard Hendel

The University of Iowa Press is a member of Green Press
Initiative and is committed to preserving natural
resources.

Printed on acid-free paper

ISBN-13: 978-1-58729-860-8
ISBN-10: 1-58729-860-0
LCCN 2009933597

For my father and my mother

It is the third commonness with light and air,
A curriculum, a vigor, a local abstraction . . .
Call it, once more, a river, an unnamed flowing,

Space-filled, reflecting the seasons, the folk-lore
Of each of the senses; call it, again and again,
The river that flows nowhere, like a sea.

—*Wallace Stevens, "The River of Rivers in Connecticut"*

CONTENTS

ACKNOWLEDGMENTS

All my gratitude and love to Stephanie Anderson. These poems would not have been written without her.

Thanks to the Bread Loaf Writers' Conference, Lucie Brock-Broido, Michael Collier, Phil Cordelli, Steven Cramer, Michael Dickman, Timothy Donnelly, Mark Doty, Okiemute Emuoyibo, the Fine Arts Work Center in Provincetown, Jack Gethen, Shafer Hall, Kristoffer Harris, Matt Hart, Matthew Henriksen, Richard Howard, Thomas Hummel, Spencer Lewis, Billy Merrell, Jason Nickerson, Michael Schiavo, Arthur Sze, Rosanna Warren, Dean Young, and Matthew Zapruder.

Grateful acknowledgment to the editors of the journals where versions of these poems first appeared: *Boston Review*: "The Greenness of Grass Is a Positive Quality"; *Cannibal*: "Each H (I)," "Each H (II)," "Each H (III)," "Each H (IV)," "Each H (V)"; *Colorado Review*: "Goodnight Lung"; *Cutbank*: "The curtains are"; *Denver Quarterly*: "Of Deadish New England Towns Sups the Incandescence," "Photography Doesn't Exist," "A Uselessness of Amadons"; *Fou*: "A Discrete or Continuous Sequence of Measurable Events Distributed in Time"; *H_NGM_N*: "Pass-Pass, or All My Pulses"; *LIT*: "Mum, Wag"; *Modern Review*: "Cognitive Burr"; *New England Review*: "Archipelago This, Archipelago That," "Uncomfortable Hand"; *New Review of Literature*: "North Meadows"; *Pool*: "A Clean Shirt," "A mountain is," "Each H (VI)," "Each H (XI)" (excerpt); *Tin House*: "Each H (VII)," "Each H (VIII)"; *Used Cat*: "Quotes from the Hartford Poems"; *VOLT*: "Nine at Nine."

Special thanks to the editors of H_NGM_N B__KS, Octopus Books, and Ugly Duckling Presse, who published versions of these poems in the following chapbooks, respectively: *Advice for Young Couples*, *Goodnight Lung*, and *Each H*.

ONE

EACH H (I)

I could not sound like anyone but me,
not like who's interested in more than
where we worry, where we were

worried how to call that righteous, when
my father says we say
righteous call; I could not sound

like anyone, but wanted to
myself sound convinced
it was easy like I got this, don't

stress what's easy like the expression
"how it was all we could do
not to go down to" the piers,

see there are piers, we
understand their general function, but
how to specifically have at

them, well that them's the heart of what
we have not yet learned, such as
why the city seems both (see there

someone who decided to see
the city) the means of its rivers and like
in my interior, where what seems

holy is not by the decoration, but
that I had not chosen them (lamps,
blinds, furniture) myself.

OF DEADISH NEW ENGLAND TOWNS SUPS
THE INCANDESCENCE

It was always different after there were no moments
it was always different after. Now that we are not this
bridge, but these bridges, no one has anywhere to go
other than the store everybody will live on is Jackie
in track pants. Jackie in track pants has a leg around
the soda machine is empty, Jackie. Can we ask you
to know us like sports radio? A morning commentary
figures prominently when one hasn't been to sleep
after every situation in the bar ends with the ice-
cold window, watching one Honda without another.
Doesn't this feel like when drowsy and nondrowsy
come together? As one tells an opponent be quiet
all of you. Disconnected the clock was supposed to
be how Brass thinks he's going to change the stock
is spoiled. Can there be no restaurant? I don't know
you from venison, but if that is the bunk, then this
is the bunk, and which is too many voices to ask?
Our town is these streets were here before it was
decided where the streets would be. Don't move
them. Don't fix them. Would you wish to fix us
you would understand we aren't for it. Every time
I run my hand through my hair, more of my hair
comes with my hand whether or not that is a new
thought is almost how I am pleased to think so.
We are not this bridge and we are not these bridges.
We are not this town is brighter than we have
gotten up before we were this become light.

EACH H (II)

We are for the park, as we are for
enjoying its proximity to how
enjoying it for itself, as a park, is our

sign we are clearly thinking. On a tangent
as often as of two minds, but
then, perhaps, also another, and yet,

like pillows, I always feel I would be
more, if I could have more, which
makes me ask what gives us

over to giving ourselves, don't end.
Don't structure. If structure
is over, we could have had it

done. Like the seriousness become
a better secret as a secret
will gain more for it going on. From it

we would become strangers better
exchanging quarters in
the station, or elevator home to

my interaction with a mother asking her
child a question I happily
answered. We are so happy to know

something. We forget our place. How
winning has more
feeling. Then we count the ways.

NORTH MEADOWS

There were no rods for where we were showing her the consideration or too cold telling her the difference was a little more ghetto than anyone gets to keep.

The fish market used to be I'm not sure how hard it is to remember what was where when landmarks must be somewhat the same.

Downtown was to walk her through which is the kind of brass we were too much to own any of it.

There was carpeting went across the sidewalk with a hand in my pocket is the way I am the one carrying it.

And by then it was best to take Homestead turned bulletproof or the carbon paper into an exterminator painted BE SAFE LEAVE THE KILLING TO US.

The feeling better than watching the window over Bridgeport and told her Waterbury but the sound was a real Bridgeport over the fuck I'm from.

Carbon paper hung under construction somewhere is open though and she wanders makes a good picture of who looked twice just wanted to bum a cigarette.

Downtown was to bring her and set us where we thought we were going to be this plaza on top of ourselves never asking why she had come.

Or we were still there and knew how it was who came up to your window and what you could tell the difference went into the line of the fish market's been closed for years.

And by then the sidewalks were all carpeting even twice as long as I remember evenly placed was carbon paper with her on the rods still.

EACH H (III)

If there weren't close-minded people,
who would love the action
like this fellow here has his hair to

practice. Blond as an angel
food cake. Food cake? Food cake,
he said, but was not hungry, not

tempted, completely set with glasses.
Well, giving him those
flips his hair like a suggestion (no

longer than the corner of your eye)
nodding, note what
folds the location (a laundromat, or all

movement) into making your suspicion
logical. How we remember to
speak like at a dinner table, saying this

is holy as not me who set it. Note a tree
works its bark into the lattice-
work works itself into the bark. Note

the unattended vehicle will be cedar
as often as cement, will flee
as the fence goes at whether

we can keep together as "we hear"
jars back "I meant" better
not to leave the container open.

QUOTES FROM THE HARTFORD POEMS

That was tri-state, like Jersey.

That was at least drugs never make me buy them dinner.

That was don't feel bad, buddy, you just got pinned by one of the top fighters in the NHL.

This is the sort of place where you bring your own.

That was I alone am to blame for mine was folly.

That was the only ears that can ever hear one's secrets are one's own.

That was I see you spinning and spinning never idle a moment, but thrifty and thoughtful of others.

That was the unspoken word is capital.

That was he no believe me.

This is the second time this has happened since we moved here. We need to move somewhere else.

This is who wore baggy jeans, but wasn't into thuggery.

That was I never pulled a living body out of the river.

This is depression as mostly the result of not drinking enough water.

That was well, if, for whatever reason, one of us were to turn into a vampire, because of her books, we'd know how to relate to the other vampires.

This is Okie? I'm Okie! Okie? No, I'm Okie, what's your name?

This is joy! Joy! Joy!

That was On Incline Accelerate to Maintain Speed.

That was don't worry, buddy, I'm not going to let anyone shoot you.

EACH H (IV)

And look at those soccer players
looking for Stamford. Could
Stamford have ever seemed the

attractive option before passing
it became regular like this
knee in my back, I don't like

it, but that it is there is something
I can recognize the value of
being familiar with what's close to

you. You know what's buried in
the chest of me could
be my bright new self, or night

soccer without the neighborhood
looking, even waking
despite how the players are running

like running is breathing more than
closing a distance. This
where you couldn't see your

hand, but felt there was rain filling
it, rain warm as this couldn't
really be what was in front of us.

TOUCHES THE HELICOPTER

If I allowed myself to smell corduroy, I would say it smells like urine, but I could say anything when corduroy is pink. Sheik came by, said *How you expect to smell anything with no flowers*. I listen, and take busy to mean wondering what overwhelming would do to my sense of how to turn back to the linoleum after taking gray for blue. Still, I'll decide which tube is scentless.

What's wrong with a patch of fabric? Floating in your pocket, folded. If I made a hole, I could sew it over, but won't while my fingers sweat. I can't say I've gripped a knuckle in years.

Train; three times a month to realize I am appropriate in my seat.

Sheik gets regular. He brings the paper and onions. We discuss too much for me to let him past the screen. Finally, I don't know why nothing happened. Or, he doesn't leave home and the paper comes subscription. I lost my silver and won't split onions with teeth.

People are pulled places for not wanting to go. I remember my business is to keep feet under the seat before me. My regular aisle is as filthy as my regular row. Across, a man puts fingers in his shirt, bites his collar. The ways people treat their clothes.

It should have been ten years ago I found six cans of coin I didn't know I hid in the garage.

An old woman looks like a small cousin of mine, crosses her ankles, and goes to sleep with her mouth open. Outside, the grass is gray, or a blue hill. I have to hold my knee to keep my hand still. She's wearing a pink scarf under a boy's winter coat.

I come back regular as I leave, but Sheik refuses to admit he's silent. Busy, so he can't smell print.

Numbers and letters on the end of the shell. It doesn't feel like anything.
I say this, and the train continues to remind me where we are going to be
stranger and left alone.

The girl came by while they were landing, said *It's empty. We're only high
enough to send people.*

Left the car running to free the door. Or, because the children climb
porches, everyone should have games. I won't believe in number when we
have further than I thought we'd go. Through the screen, I hear an acre of
high grass. Think I won't face it. Even with hours. I watch it gold. Enough,
a difference in gray and blue. Then I saw Sheik in the grass, red plaid with
nothing to tell me.

EACH H (V)

Something to be said for how long
what has been growing
along the road, has been growing

along a road, must change how
it grows. Louder then,
when you see the sign GUNS

has an actual white picket fence
around it. Around where
the little blue houses start

everywhere with what they collect
the position between
arbitrary and how long has it been

since you were assigned some-
thing? Look, they have
a harbor, and where the dock is

gone someone left the poles in.
Something to
edges rests, settled

between poles, one feels this
preference
like being still doesn't worry

us, this is what we have
chosen, to value this
looks like we have chosen before.

A DISCRETE OR CONTINUOUS SEQUENCE OF
MEASURABLE EVENTS DISTRIBUTED IN TIME

I had not approached, but could have prepared a distance
just like interested in crossing
                              put some muscle to blue
paint on this porch looks like tin, the branches cross over
makes more than I can keep the house shut
                                        sooner or
neighbor, we're going to decide who owns the tree, sweeps
the playoffs
              I have to tell you I cared about hockey
games were what I couldn't bear
                                  which is what this is now
whether or not I am more the man to understand them

I have prepared the onions in quarters
                                  with horseradish
you can never tell what won't work
                                  before experiments
with you for me including my mother finds my father's
grandmother's diary notes that she is wondering
                                        what this
century will bring her an answer no one was expecting
anything else
              eating the peas with my fingers I am just
close enough to know they will run out has everything to
do with changes in their texture
                            it is the distinction

between the rain is on the roof and is it morning makes me
notice where this light is that refrigerator
                                  I have left
strawberries mold in how many I have left

                              I am afraid
I am like this all the time for a reason
                              I am afraid is
something I am not going to know how to tell what it is
from everything is a box-cut of we don't know
                                        the orange
from light
          from light we measure is everything here
                                        is not
everything was selected whether or not
          is everything right.

THE CURTAINS ARE

eager to speak with glass-green their demonstration
that welcome colors the passage of hello to
hello the wood you have come to in just to feel how
thick felt velvet as learning to examine fingers
know who touches begins to resemble how touching
a hole in the wall becomes you vulnerable
when sitting back to answer what used to be here
was a mantle of considerate fireplace discussion
about the headlines covering introduction further
than this may not be the time everything was clean
and ours for five more minutes until appointment
arrived after the meeting seemed to be over how
that's a strange order to hurry along with baskets
show the way they were woven palms sway as
reminders that this was the border and could it
expect what greeting came for.

LIKE AN EVENING

Comfort is not what keeps me here
deciding I cannot like my seat as much
as what it means to topple
out and onto where it would be difficult
to separate me from airport
when it is instead the plane
taking off; I could go several ways
with how best to put everything
should come together is no longer available
now that I am aware I govern
what makes what I govern
differ not from how it must seem
like discomfort
staying where you wish to be.

Were I to ask where you were staying
would that be what moves
our discussion beyond whether repetition
has more to offer than repetition
will be enough when I say
it has been enough is not enough
is now and much
like I remember drinking milk
is just one of the many tasks
I am often unable to accomplish
as a result of mistaking seeing the necessity
for the act itself; the first possibility
we do not know how
backward we determine ourselves.

Welcome to the hallway door!
Have I forgotten where I was
supposed to be sleeping and not
paying attention to how much
there is to worry about
my room, if it will be warmer
now that I believe production
of a second person simply by
speaking to them is no more
unreasonable than for us
to assume aspects of a personality
exist by our requiring them to
have less to do with our reasons
the more often we remake them.

Accountable could mean to imagine
withholding as an option
rather than transition into who knows
who to be kind to, why I would want
a pet to clasp. It—he—will not stay
still. I explain my lap is no more
used to being held than the one
heaving interaction with reason
behind not everyone wrecks
the possibilities for a relationship
this new morning may
develop with did you hear
how to handle the interruption: make
what you have more you are able.

And then went down to Sam's Quality
Verité, had a comfy malt between
shelves. Delicious, and could not see
how unappeasable we would be
after the parkway gardens, where
dogs gather from gutters
photographs of their owners in joy,
distress. Expressions we examined
and felt what we could from
distress was more
common and most like those
hours I misunderstood how to quit
pain in my bladder was why
I brought you cup on cup of water.

Lost just losing sight of choosing
to see everything at once
as what directs us is not choice,
is a result of what is there. And if
I said I cannot be present the hour
before, I am present the hour
after, then why in both can I not be
quiet? If someone just showed me
settle down, I would
not louder than before
and longer after
find the absence of the lovely
day, or register
the choice as now and choosing.

From the deep fissures of the Freestyle
Amber Room, the Yew-tree bursts!
Make proud your mossy
contribution, you educate the leap
by you are bounded. Is
the peak well read? Then climber
must concede a climb is not
entertaining us more than who could
have known the weather
would be so pleasant. Cooler than
expected a chance for the breezy
cloud of pollen enveloping
our mouths open
when we disturb with recreation.

Cold where could have waited
for what would wash up
to be what could not be cleaner
than what burdens you
have your own display
was careful to appear various
with its location and time
was nothing but as regular as
I have been looking for you
without discussion
I was aware the moment you
would believe the moment it was
the bed washed up warm
almost as we are what returns us.

Comfort what beached the early
rocks smoothed growth into
this silence is neither
expected nor rest, but like
the movement one notices
not everything
washes up to shore. Somehow
already between the sand
and unexpected subject we have
come to what would have been
here if we had not
come thinking there was nothing
here learning
we do not decide our subject to.

Before each presence is our institution
one could always learn
forward disappears similar
to Location is everything
as irregular as you
have a wall settling in you? Would you
stay close or more
like an evening
degenerate to why I would
drop the sentence
is a distraction that comes
when one fixes
a solid as the solid we should not be
asking for weight from sight.

Warmth not unlike what keeps
the performance
eyes and lids like ached and like
cupped for remainder
to be not taken
as exit. We will have again
neither yard of padded metal
nor cool sheet that ends
beyond appreciation
of what around us
deserves us no better
sleep outside a home
noise returns
what we want from it.

Salt much more than decaying
sounds like never failing
is speaking possibility
for the prose holding you
is wild apart
from your turn on door. Also
less reasonable than what it was
to serve the moment
before shouting will no wrong
heard windows corridor you
to belief unwaking is
unrelenting as I would not
anticipate the effects
your finger closes over mine.

Who can see more furniture
in the future of this light
or that disappearance must be
like so much speaking by the river
I am asked to remember
questioning as what cuts
a figure was
read as me cut out of frame
by fact of absence, not
the same as what necessary
glass comes to bank
our looking further into
why we are gone
before we know what left.

Comfort is what burned exactly where
you were, then that left
guessing you would like your rest
to mean take less. I was unable
or constant as rain dispersing
lenses into sewers. Where
was the caution to enter with
instructions for an hour
unaware was lying the hour
down or down to what could simply
be called constant
was living quieter with time after
we were never sure before
each presence is our last.

EACH H (VI)

If it was a trip, well who was on it? There
were lots. No, one. No one
was on it, they were after it. If they were

after him, they won't find him in the wind.
How's that possible? This is New
England. You're saying there's no wind?

No, not that, but what I think is that
it wasn't a trip. Why not?
I wasn't on it. You weren't on it? We

weren't on it. If we're not on it, then
it's not a trip? It's not
a trip. What is it? Forget it, what's

this? This is us. Well, then don't we feel
like some kind of destination's
been reached? If that's it, then something

must come after. Yeah, he comes after.
You mean, after us. He's after us?
No, he's us. Well, then he's in the wind.

PASS-PASS, OR ALL MY PULSES

Let us acknowledge there is an audience
or that the passage being read *a bird*

taps on a model home in Northern California
has caught hold of the first three rows of

warranting a lecture with their little bags
of looking forward from who they were

here to be onto that portion of dedicated
reminiscence they expected to include

the story of a rug delayed its fragility partly
by a pair of clotheslines, but more by chairs

where who could have a delicate thought
after hours of those around us think this

vibration would be better worded tuning
as we each have an inch of knee busying

itself closer to those changes in an attitude
that becomes more collective the less it is

accepted. Much like an unfortunate sort
of speaker. He has left his something to

happen at home, where he will carry back
what he was trying to accomplish being

too trying for an audience less aware of
what they came for than the way in which

was partnered an answer to their question
of had they even come for anything at all.

ARCHIPELAGO THIS, ARCHIPELAGO THAT

Went out to where the leaves spread scuttlefist.
Neva. Tsars. Took the canary you hid at home
where I would find him & had hoped I wouldn't

ask, would take him, hand him (early, empty)
but how he wouldn't, for miserable, for bleak-
broke, fly. Soldiers came demanding. Tried

Dutch. Tried Finnish. Brought out, I mentioned
you & bird. Here was some incompetent
morning of gestures & useless task. They took

my coins, didn't linger or flinch for my bother.
Bird on my finger. Flickless bird. Featherstayed.
You would be up soon. What have I ever been?

A USELESSNESS OF AMADONS

Asked how I ended up breaking into
the high school. Perfectly, myself

dragged a gym-horse to a classroom,
said to it *Something wrong with how*

you keep my adrenaline away from me.
What a thing to do, dividing myself

between a piece of gym equipment
borrowed & a mind gone off when

no one told to answer. & yes, knew
we were distinct. & yes, still climbed

my arms around & hung under gap
at the middle of it where wouldn't

fit what wanted like birds outside
surgical in how they hide the night.

EACH H (VII)

I could not sound like anyone to anyone,
but often meant to almost (as
rocking is from weaving) sound

local, as there should be more
local, I started saying here, how-
ever I sounded saying

I can be here again, saying it over
in a way so it piled, in a way
piling, as we cannot see it

ending, where it is from, the reason for
it is in fact frightening
to hear so much anywhere in anyone.

UNCOMFORTABLE HAND

If I were to describe the degree to which
my pupils dilate, would anything more

be forgiven? Without an unmanageable
mistake, the day doesn't happen. On

the train (blackly barefoot) this swaddle
of sag wearing wet so I ask *Is it begging*

if it's grunted? Or, a lady toothless says
Essays, sure. But let me get a chicken bone.

I've come to understand a person mentions
they don't know what will happen next

to mean they are unsatisfied with their
previous. When I broke the window

latch, when I jammed the door, when I
took to cusp, when I opened in my lip.

MUM, WAG

You see I am here & not there
out those thunder. Minneapolis

is near & dreadfully sorry abt dog.
All masters do the last 100 yards

before a river & the quarry where
people & water washing was ice.

Tuesday was obscene labour
& better to spend in bed until

monstrously he banked, obliged
to bob to deepest of knockt.

About initials & dashes, sounds
Here, Cathedrals—a cardboard

where once three movements of
dearest John taking the darkness.

NORTH OF PROVIDENCE

Listen to the heaters & think
if they'd rise to the ceiling, we'd wish
all our objects to lift themselves

as noisily. How we live in a world
that moves without attention. Put
bells to walls. Then don't listen. Go out

into isn't that just a brighter not
thinking things through? Yes, or it's what forgives
our not knowing how a lawn exists

after snow's been packed across our eyes.
Let's move for one more instance of it
mattering what we thought; these people

sit on runways, cicadas into windows.

PHOTOGRAPHY DOESN'T EXIST

My pants barely hold together & you
want me to know something. All I said

was the television provides much more.
Turn there. Wooden motorcycles & set

of someone else's getaway. News has
maps of Georgia & stills from weather.

I have no money. I don't know why bees
make love, but I'm sorry about the storm.

Thing now is to decide what to do with
all the water. I'd make airplanes so we

could expose distance as fraud. Hartford
has people everywhere: mountains,

prairies, Los Angeles. What do they say?
Where's a tomato garden? I'll bury one.

EACH H (VIII)

And again blood is the only word
we cannot alter the way we
feel about it. That is not legs, faces, pants,

breathing. That you cannot breathe is unlike
when the water in the shower
will not get hot, nonetheless

the water in the shower will not get hot,
and I would like a word for that
sensation. Now

and again I feel limits, but simply the wine
merges how we keep
lit with numb as a screw won't

go into its hold, led into this feeling,
we liked the feeling,
we would have gone simple

for it, for how we felt there
is a word (countable/
uncountable) like breath-also-breath.

GOODNIGHT LUNG

Planes move their sound on us & believe
walls explode, but haven't & don't wonder

yet. Went to the middle of things, which is
where we edge on strange future. Anyone

thinks tobacco too costly leaves a different
taste behind than me. Here's a street looks

like other streets & I have no idea what
fills trees. How do we find a thing which

isn't concerned enough with us to hide?
I put my hand on the wall, wonder if

I'm wearing what's right for the weather.
None of the children have bicycles. Even

our apples are mined for pits. Chance
may yet provide us boxes. I'd close mine.

THE BARBER'S FINGERS MOVE OCTOBER

If I watch two white cats play in a window
which is not the window I should be watching

when a window I watch through is the window
I should be washing, then we know today

is going to be a difficult to listen to all his talking
when his shirts are open, when his face is

pulsing. Would anyone like to see my thumbs
lonely, or growing from one leg to the next

brownstone overflowing with people unprepared
for how happily I'm going to be making lunch

look like a portrait of milk next to seventy-two
days of tomato soup, each peppered

with less cooking makes for opportunity to see
my foot pressed against Grant's Tomb

which is just to say mustache. But
could landmarks be what I've been neglecting

to mention, how unproductive never leaving
the house might actually be what you were

meaning? I'm sorry. Sometimes listening takes
stealing a bus, or finding a way to parking lots

large enough in which to fishtail.
A reason for snow having not come. This year

is going to be a good idea becomes better
after sharing it with strangers, or settle down

before you worry yourself into a newspaper
subscriber who won't take the time to more

than rinse a mug. Isn't water what we were after
all I can't remember, but believe as a child

I was a vision of not really the strongest swimmer
on his hands, collecting grass for filters because *enough*

with the ceiling fan it's summer Sam no one but me will
believe you are a robot who prefers a beach in tight

khakis with no belt because it's back home holding
his project in rotation, which is sort of like me

now, see how I can make my chair stop or keep
my chair spinning, either way I must be up for something

has made one white cat try hard his face against
the glass until a vein appears which, followed, leads

us back to apparently my bicycle was taken off
the shelf. What if I rode it with my knees spread down

the four flights of stairs out this building
into the street without checking the cars' side

mirrors for if I still pedal with my mouth open?
Better you leave it too precarious in the doorway

for me to follow after the door is knocked
by the wind from a window I will open now

that it's safe to say this has been a full morning
of staring through the half-reflection of my face

figuring out how it would sound
to understand every word you were saying.

EACH H (IX)

That it could sound like him.
That it could sound like him
sounding like he knew

what he sounded like. That it
could sound like he knew
what it was to sound like some-

one, or something he knew
was that it
couldn't sound more

like what it was then when
it sounded like more
than what it was. Like how

we all sounded saying that
was it, but that was it
again, and then wasn't this more

it anyway, or just it with more
people, more to say
that it could sound like people.

EACH H (X)

That it could sound like us?
How's that a question.
Which part?

It has parts?
If it's like us.
You mean we're parts?

I thought we said we were him.
No, we said he's us.
You said he's us.

It was a different situation.
You said it was "the wind."
I'm saying it was a situation.

~~~

Say it was a situation. I'll say that
makes a situation. Oh, like
what makes the French. Makes

the French what? The French what
has that presence. In what
situation? You mean

what presence. Now this to burn
through. Well, I would have
too, but for the open propane

containers. Are they still containers
if they're open? There's a law. Of
containers? Just for the open ones.

~~~

I hope it's more for the condition.
Like treatment?
Treatment's so humane.

I always think they mean human.
Human like condition?
I said condition.

You said situation.
I would have too, but for the result.
The situation is a result.

No, a container.
That's to say it was open.
I thought it was his, like presence.

~~

I said he had this presence.
Of mind?
Yes, mind.

To what?
To sound.
To sound like what?

More like here.
Oh, like talk.
You mean talk in a movie?

Yes, a movie.
What kind?
The kind he liked talk in.

~~

The kind where his talking
during them
was like his talk

to himself, maybe, but never
out loud, actually, it was
more he liked how

he liked it, less
that he never actually did it
himself. So, he knew

what he was doing. You mean
talking? No,
here, like in a movie.

FOUR

EACH H (XI)

Are we here he always has to ask
Those questions with that language
What language was that what you were

Thinking no wearing regardless
The car's been brought
Around when we were arriving

With when we were leaving is where we are
As if there'd be anywhere else
To have it they couldn't have it

They couldn't have it or couldn't
Take it you take it or we'll take it
But I don't know where

He was going to think that of this
This was dinner or that was
Language their language his language

Who else it belonged to
Like everyone knows everyone knows
Everyone knows and nobody cares

It was almost over but don't you
Know where we are it doesn't matter
It'll matter when it's over when it's over

We'll know where everyone
Lets their congratulations to your talent
Proceed you

This afternoon to whiteness and to
Witness what we must make
A deal of Sharon

Venturing without cake into winter parties
Where she likes to brush the feathers back
Likes the exuberant accounting of

An idyllic life
Was never why you hid your heart
Why your heart's with us over pools the pool-

Boy hasn't drained them so we let them
Be frozen and yet expect roses
Lips swimmers pinks wispy purples blue

Of course after our amusement
There's a statement made by you
Appropriate to your position

The company you keep can employ
Exit now we would be grateful
As it's gotten late we must be

Heading before the door opens
On the moment after a little sad
For our shaking glad to do it with

I believe it was Massachusetts
Has several highways crossing forests
Makes me consider what is not

Crossing freshness or a scent
Resembling freshness
Again as order the redness resumes

The sky where it can be
Presence and my father to photograph it
Not from the car but who is in it

Not our faces but braced against the heater
Sometimes that steady
Sometimes that was as difficult

To know what to say as what to say
Was significant as significance
Becomes not what but that you

Assign heat we can have an automobile
Christmas oh girl
Could my humming oh girl

But be hear it human condition
On the condition it was me who had
Synth slick as our automobile

Christmas told her be here with drum
Loop the human condition
You heard my father saying hold the ladder

Light the tree the diner parking lot
Is on the street to Christmas
With the heat what's on is piano oh girl

Humming it human condition was how
Here there on the coast by the sea
Heat is piano to the automobile to

Me to move with interest in thought
Is how everything is a surface passing
Me to overcrowded platform human

Kindness in the grooves of where I am well-
Formed like children in the gallery
One has a place to know they are quietly amassing

Like you what pushed me
Off the mat past the porch supports
There there many in their weak passes

Will ask is it us that we are not alone
Or always with you with you always
What winds tighter causes the delay

More like a trolley than we have our
Plaza only when you enter it
Either we pause here or notice later

Rain on our arms in our sweaters
Matches laces we have tied the Inter-
Faith Cathedral to Community Road

With Community Road Extension
Where I am the only one walking for
My activities to be less the sense

There were more men than women
At the table or under the marigolds
Was whoever pays attention to

Fragrance anymore or invitations
The color of paint feathering below the tool-
Shed across Januaries like levels in cement

Always in the shade or an office
Possibly a variant on workshop still
To have lost the apartment to have given up everything

Except a little sugar in the coffee
Thought that made it more like "ice cubes
A treat" his mother said and he believed her

But wouldn't have known how to discuss
That or when every choice became listless
As quite a series of films were

Better than he was going to like
Like these people how he felt not even
A hint of surprise at things he honestly couldn't

Have predicted they would say
This after giving up was interesting
Lips won't stay wet even

With the evening pleased with the art
Well more decorations for
At home with don't care won't labor

This when the usual party becomes
Fascinated by the blizzard out to see
Snow keep voices from echoing off

The minor peaks of western Massachusetts
Oh what hasn't he thought of weather
Oh why doesn't he hop into some car

Fill the compartments with lottery
Tickets people are so excited sometimes
He can hardly name a chain of islands

From Aleutian to Elizabeth gather
Something fateless as realizing
A day more like others than itself is over

FIVE

WHAT WAS DRAINED IS FLOODED AND AFTER COMES

moving harder than plastic
becomes not these legs used to be made for

fingers tracing from when the quilt warmed
them without seeming

unnecessary. Friends, we are not yet
but coming closer to now we will quietly

move to the back of the porch
without alerting the street at how we are

afraid it will say *What was drained is flooded*
and after there will be nothing

but to build a replica of where we were
when we did not keep worthwhile worthwhile.

. . .

And the drained is nothing without seeming plastic
after are we afraid of the porch is unnecessary

worthwhile. The quilt becomes a replica quietly
flooded the street of but we did to, are we made for.

And not from them when, but there now will we
not moving say back at friends. Alerting what comes

yet not how what used to be, will, when these fingers
keep closer than after we were was to move legs

where will it be was warmed, flooded. Worthwhile
tracing drained, coming without to build harder.

A MOUNTAIN IS

where a lake extends beyond the trees, directions are larger
than this document is discursive, and could be narrower, briefly,
but later stakes, in assortment, turn order no more tenable
than this lake is a collection located somewhat shady
in northern New Hampshire. Are you with me? Here or there
our excuses are only for each other to make something.
A river? By river, we say, this river looked like a hundred years
before anyone said something so foolish. I am for understanding
landscape as more impressive than portrait is where still
we squabble over the windows are letting in the rain, out the warm
comfortable. It's convertible. It's so soft, your sofa,
how could anyone argue over Sunday should be we have to go
back now. How welcome home garlic in the kitchen, mince
it together and when we rinse our hands it does not leave them.
What if whatever floated on the water wouldn't ripple
and still we couldn't recognize faces turn around to say
we understand flowing down to the resolution, with the ocean
it's never a surprise we cannot see faces asking were we
aware these destinations would be turning no
more necessary than directions once we know our way.

FRESH WARM

Have you noticed expressions on my face
or the ways in which recent angers
seem themselves like what comes

pleasant as commitments to sustain
the patio isn't finished, when I find
some flagstone. You find some flagstone.

I find I am not the one who is well
after misplacing caution for a flight.
Like this a train whistle. And another

when arrangement finds its function
is substantially what has been let
off this morning, or home. If I differ

time of day from location, will it be more
apparent I should be waking to
the idea that my feeling about my living

doesn't matter more with planning?
How same will always into same
uncomfortably. The decision to order

a series of overflowing meals from separate
restaurants over several days
similar in how one remembers a reason

for food. What sways between characteristic
and protest is me, or everyone
waiting for now to be more like peering

down, to rest our heads against the house,
where if didn't notice the progress
of the lawn, we would not be ourselves.

But wish to. And not know how to investigate
our loss, or what was taken
was where we were what we were after all along.

A CLEAN SHIRT

Look is there a clean shirt. But there is a clean shirt.
But there a clean shirt. Look is there a clean shirt.

Here a sentence for where we could fit it. Here how
the letters are shifting, are us become less

with invitations in the gutters we are coming to limit

our access is too much without
too much we don't have access to where we could

fit the letters are inviting us the ones shifting.

Look there is a lake after our luggage has our luggage
in mind. There is a bin available should there be a bin

available we are going to be able to. Like the lake

we are is where we are is our luggage.

Without whose help there would be no weight on him
saying without help weight on mine is

I would ask it to if I could balance.

Of course, he could juggle. He could juggle, of course,
no one expected he couldn't, but wondered more for

what he was juggling was us and our direction was us

ourselves, juggling is always a circle, of course, he, us
could not have wondered more for, of course, no one

expected he could juggle us ourselves.

Ordinarily the glasses. Or ordinarily filled, the glasses
were filled, could the glasses be filled, or now would

you please fill the glasses. Ourselves, but our access

is too much without our direction, our direction was
a sentence we could fit it there, there is a clean shirt.

But there a clean shirt. Look is there a clean shirt.

FOGHORNS

Foghorns couldn't wager right, foghorns properly. Thinking. Socialist.
Farm. You pigs. Bathing purpose, Harker, Shaughnessy. Socialist.
Few, you, regretting, nothing, reason, summer, anything leopard's
for you. Beg, although barrooms. History, thousand peasants
for your rag, father without foghorn. Sleeping upstairs
for you. Arguments. Mother suppose different, certainly upstairs
for you. Ought father suppose Mister sneaking upstairs
for you. Begun. Night. Nervous matter. Certainly weakness
forever would wages nothing without matter. Captain. Morning's
feel come mug right barrooms. Father scolding goodness
for lonely. Right father. Doctor. Doctors. Anything upstairs
for moment. Bogtrotter. Right. Without matter. Anything poorhouse
for something. Dig. Nightdress. Season children. Ignorant serpent's
friends you leg much serious matter. Medicine forgives.
Faith, love, foghorn, Cathleen, foghorn, master, anything worships.
Forgive you, fog, night forgotten matters. Medicine hopeless.
Foghorn, for right, bashful, introduced different becoming upstairs
for you. Foggy with jealous failure sneering serpent's
filthy hotels, Eugene, nothing, reason better boarding teachers.
Fine. How. Began. Might. Poison. Father. Ignorant. Business.
Forget no figure with forgotten tampering. Everyone poorhouse
fool to ought. Nightdress. Doctor. Doctor. Ignorant comparison
forbid you foghorn. Hush. Without mother. Anything poorhouse
fool. Poor argue. Either. Bottom. Performance. Drunken citadel's
from tower, night, night-long. Dowson, waiter, Schopenhauer, atheists,
fools, your degenerates, perhaps, without, dinner, haunting, memories.
Father noble. Might mother. Poison doctor. Morphine bargains.

Found morphine, night night, poison matter, shouldn't poorhouse.
Found. Work. Tightwad. Nothing. Doctors. Bracer. Stinking poorhouse
feel your hugging with lesson. Unlearn bargains. Machinist
for nothing. Iago. Night rundown spattering, towering, craziness.
For. Got. Fog. Lighthouse. Doctor's. Orders. Drunken. Patients
for you. Lights without hollow dancers concerning upstairs
for. Joke. Bughouse. Night. Performing. Proper. Everyone troubles
finished. Now highest, mother, follow bastard, certainly, brothers
for you. Highbrow. Nothing. Doctors. Doctors, judgment, mistakes,
fake. Look. Ought. Hath. Performance. Loafer. Argument. Knuckles
find how sang, sighing poison, mother explained enormous.

MY HUMMEL IS SELF-PROPELLED ARTILLERY

The engines say the engines are not driving
questions into a line behind the shop
of a butcher who fingers his hands

without designs for their chances. But
almost in favor. Of the same was to touch.
As to make room for. Which asks?

When you wanted to offer on the table.
Or, when it was drawn with the elements
of an explanation. Can you steer it?

And to where must we go for you to know
what it is requirement is still
herding us into tanks we can take

Germany. Anywhere, let us have green slopes
go blank, then blurry, then what put
if not a pause in the seat sounds like

pedestal. Spite a hornet setting housefire.
In that light will become clearer
our citrus, like character revealing its choice.

The engines say the engines are not gloves
but might be if how we wear them
was chassis, to be held there were pushed.

NINE AT NINE

There were ninety-seven. New York   and then, went down to the ship

in our struggle for responsibility   from here I see. A single red cloud,

I have been wanting to write *you*   *be happy if the wind inside the orchard*

over two months elapsed before   *where are you going to-night?* To-night

I was captured by the fascist   but I do not want to see him again,

to think that Amaryllis had grown old   away. Under the skin of his neck

starved men are celebrating   (apologize whenever you find it convenient)

who cry, outraged, *Lord when did we see?* You   itself, the infinite resonance of its sound

such as *lie smothered in grass by San Vitale*   reverberating within four tiled walls.

She explained to Eloise who had come   there can be but the one Sordello,

what we do and think is filled   as he flings lath and plaster, or cleared.

Probably you expect me to meditate,   walk only among plants

he took with him to Fontenay.   There, where the vines cling crimson on the wall.

Then, the lorry stopped and we saw   the thief and the victim with equal gravity

before she gave him time enough to wink,   start choking, frozen, crazy. With fear,

a trifle, a sunflower opening,   are you really in Nazi Germany?

Water moving like thoughts   mourning. Plays are called music

and brought back the levies   designing her own Christmas. Cards:

Selena's father made them or something   and there were not those girls there. Was one face

few works, outside the great works, of classical   —argue? They don't ask for much.

Perhaps you wrote a letter and forgot   the instruments of the thick trees. And sweeps

that restricted idiom with its limited: *long centuries have come.* And gone

I am not. Sleepy or more. Accurately   genug für die Suppe gemacht.

So friends (dear friends) remember if you will   of dislike, of the trouble involved,

a hoopoe, or two,   a fellow at Harvard called McCreary,

the farmer set off for the barn,   the terrible mixture of castrato. And faun

eyes floating in dry dark air   spoke to him, but he didn't answer her the rest of the afternoon. Weather   hear me Cadmus. Of golden prows,

the elements of the ultimate condition, do   the clapboards clean and now

all laws, morals, and rewards are   you know, but you're fearless. All the same

they informed their master   through broken walls and gray

around us; everything is hostile.   If one could only cry

that outraged *Faith has entered in his name*.   The lamps were smoking

to the flowing ooze of a gutter; see them float away   not sure whether he has mailed it

in their stalls. Suppose even the ear of wheat,   a chaste abstraction, but to a life of art

and Cairels was (of Sarlat)   the courage to wind it and find out.

Mrs. Snell having finished the cleaning   down in the viae stadae toga'd the crowd and arm'd

relation of the artistic. Cannon to the imagination   under rags, I come back to my dooryard:

the water's fine and so are we   but cuts. Across the empty hours

he had bought Moreau's two masterpieces   and he was, always. Quietly arrayed,

they have to worry about acquiring.   The hurricane starts up again

to make us wish that we were in his place   similar to the life of a monk

almost more breathed than heard   affectionately—

and fall onto already-fallen leaves;   this is the origin of light and shade;

"Se pia" —Varchi   have to help him carry the sails down.

THE GREENNESS OF GRASS IS A POSITIVE QUALITY

Morning was when we decided if not for the grass rising then wind shifted the film even as your fingers said wind can't shift film inside a camera.

What inside the camera couldn't be shifted from grass rising to a tree without the film shifting the tree black we decided was purple with light between your fingers.

Was the tree light between your fingers?

Or was the curtain along the windowsill how we didn't measure the width was where the wind was coming from?

The moment the wind was light inside the curtain was when we couldn't keep the grass from rising inside the camera.

Or where the grass was rising inside the camera was when we couldn't see the film was shifting light between your fingers.

The moment the tree was light between your fingers was how we ask could the curtain have kept us fastened from becoming weight?

How were we to know where we were morning wasn't the same as leaving an outline we could picture a yard as the width we asked to carry weight.

We counted that morning as the curtain shifting to grass which suggests any measurement is always time.

We were dark or unmeasured before the morning was the moment you were both the grass and shifting the camera between your fingers.

There is no measurement for how nothing could be morning after the camera shifting grass was light between your fingers.

COGNITIVE BURR

Take down the fresh idea I would not approximate
like papers and they are pretty. Floored
by the ambient clean is how one should decide their

thoughtfulness by making the mistake
with the nets was only building a net. Were we
available to each other with our off-hours

from possible designs would mean we had
a notebook. Or utility. I find reasonable utility
in the exposed geology of the Canyonlands

area. This regards my wishing for wonderful gorges.
But who wouldn't wonder where
the singing was coming from the people would

stop the song not over might be moving toward
a new octave discovered I am one for drilling.
From here on we move continuing to where

it means pleasure by distribution, or it disturbs
me to continue so I continue to distribute
what I have thought of for only a moment

and still it is worth a moment more. What cones
would mark where I had the first idea
to place them. Of course, we could also

go to the theater of places we would have
talked about going where we are
going to find them. This is the scene for the less-

than-casual gardener. The gardener of import
is not the gardener of intrigue
which is why we have levels rewarding the non-

native English speaker works for a mapmaker
who strikes that those are not
the phrases I would use cultural to assume

each country has made these phrases for
us. We must press the gazebo into our
hearts. And of that engraving we will need

someone's saving to be what held us up
over where the water was
losing control of the time we set

to tour the grounds. This is a large estate.
That is a great house for how
we are going to live there. Perfectly knit

with a mind for our work and at desiring
the fountain which takes us
first to the quarry of brown and black

marble. The endless series of individual swirls.
I could have stood miles forever.
Or sat in a chair comfortable fake leather

unused to being placed in an expanse it would
slowly shift my weight downward
where one may remember there should be window-

boxes if what we are building is home. It is
what else are we capable of
moving and stopping the right thought seems

almost contrary to what was decided was there
is a cleanliness comes after
one has asked for it repeatedly from the present

situation is not the situation I asked to be in
a mist that does not linger like
the moment after one is asked to now come

forward. I can be inaccurate without knowing
it is time these jurors found their own
testimony more intriguing. Or let them wait

for me to admit all our argument extends
is knowing not enough together
as the quality of this air comes by chance

labor the words with precision was how to
make me unhappy to understand.
An instrument should not know it is unlikely.

NOTES

Touches the Helicopter is in memory of Arthur Amadon and Thomas Lomento.

A Discrete or Continuous Sequence of Measurable Events Distributed in Time is a phrase taken from Charles Olson's poem "The Kingfishers," which was previously taken by Olson from the introduction to Norbert Wiener's *Cybernetics or Control and Communication in the Animal and the Machine.*

Archipelago This, Archipelago That is for Stephanie Anderson.

Mum, Wag is constructed of words and phrases taken from *We Dream of Honour: John Berryman's Letters to His Mother.*

North of Providence is for Timothy Donnelly.

"Look is there **A Clean Shirt**" is from Samuel Beckett's *Murphy.*

Foghorns applies Jackson Mac Low's diastic reading procedure to Eugene O'Neil's *A Long Days Journey into Night.*

My Hummel Is Self-Propelled Artillery is for Thomas Hummel.

The lines and phrases of **Nine at Nine** were taken as a result of a chance procedure applied to texts by J. D. Salinger, Ezra Pound, Walter Benjamin, Jane Kenyon, Robert Lowell, Eugenio Montale, Joris-Karl Huysmans, Edwin Arlington Robinson, and Primo Levi.

The Wikipedia entry for grass notes, "The grass is always greener on the other side. In this instance, **The Greenness of Grass Is a Positive Quality.**"

IOWA POETRY PRIZE AND
EDWIN FORD PIPER POETRY AWARD WINNERS

1987
Elton Glaser, *Tropical Depressions*
Michael Pettit, *Cardinal Points*

1988
Bill Knott, *Outremer*
Mary Ruefle, *The Adamant*

1989
Conrad Hilberry, *Sorting the Smoke*
Terese Svoboda, *Laughing Africa*

1990
Philip Dacey, *Night Shift at the Crucifix Factory*
Lynda Hull, *Star Ledger*

1991
Greg Pape, *Sunflower Facing the Sun*
Walter Pavlich, *Running near the End of the World*

1992
Lola Haskins, *Hunger*
Katherine Soniat, *A Shared Life*

1993
Tom Andrews, *The Hemophiliac's Motorcycle*
Michael Heffernan, *Love's Answer*
John Wood, *In Primary Light*

1994
James McKean, *Tree of Heaven*
Bin Ramke, *Massacre of the Innocents*
Ed Roberson, *Voices Cast Out to Talk Us In*

1995
Ralph Burns, *Swamp Candles*
Maureen Seaton, *Furious Cooking*

1996
Pamela Alexander, *Inland*
Gary Gildner, *The Bunker in the Parsley Fields*
John Wood, *The Gates of the Elect Kingdom*

1997
Brendan Galvin, *Hotel Malabar*
Leslie Ullman, *Slow Work through Sand*

1998
Kathleen Peirce, *The Oval Hour*
Bin Ramke, *Wake*
Cole Swensen, *Try*

1999
Larissa Szporluk, *Isolato*
Liz Waldner, *A Point Is That Which Has No Part*

2000
Mary Leader, *The Penultimate Suitor*

2001
Joanna Goodman, *Trace of One*
Karen Volkman, *Spar*

2002
Lesle Lewis, *Small Boat*
Peter Jay Shippy, *Thieves' Latin*